ideals CHRISTMAS

More Than 50 Years of Celebrating Life's Most Treasured Moments

Vol. 55, No. 6

"God bless Us, Every One!"
—Charles Dickens

IDEALS—Vol. 55, No. 6 November MCMXCVIII IDEALS (ISSN 0019-137X) is published six times a year: January, March,
May, July, September, and November by IDEALS PUBLICATIONS INCORPORATED,
535 Metroplex Drive, Suite 250, Nashville, TN 37211.
Periodical postage paid at Nashville, Tennessee, and additional mailing offices.
Copyright © MCMXCVIII by IDEALS PUBLICATIONS INCORPORATED.
POSTMASTER: Send address changes to Ideals, PO Box 305300, Nashville, TN 37230. All rights reserved.
Title IDEALS registered U.S. Patent Office.

SINGLE ISSUE—U.S. $5.95 USD; Higher in Canada
ONE-YEAR SUBSCRIPTION—U.S. $19.95 USD; Canada $36.00 CDN (incl. GST and shipping); Foreign $25.95 USD
TWO-YEAR SUBSCRIPTION—U.S. $35.95 USD; Canada $66.50 CDN (incl. GST and shipping); Foreign $47.95 USD

ISBN 0-8249-1152-0 GST 131903775

Cover Photo
HOLIDAY POINSETTIAS
Dick Dietrich Photography

Inside Front Cover
ERIK'S DELIGHT
Donald Zolan, artist
© Pemberton & Oakes
All Rights Reserved

Inside Back Cover
A CHRISTMAS PRAYER
Donald Zolan, artist
© Pemberton & Oakes
All Rights Reserved

WINTER EVENING

Sometimes a longing
   for an adequate word
Clutches my heart
As if a hand were pressed
Tight on my breast.

It is said that the Japanese
Have one word for the blue
   of the sky after rain;
A word for the fluted look
   of wind-swept grain
Down any field.

Had I word for this pale tea-rose light
Along the east before the winter night
Drops its silvered blackness on the land,
I think perhaps the hand
Clutching my heart would loose
   its desperate hold.

Must I grow old
Never able to say at all
What a winter evening says to me?
Its twilight, clear as a crystal ball,
And still
As that great star over the hill;
The blue-white shadows,
   and the rosy light,
That comes for a brief moment
   before night,
Then goes, soft-feathered
   and swift as a winging bird?
Oh, for a word!

Grace Noll Crowell

Mt. Rainier reflects on the frozen surface of Upper Tipsoo Lake in Mount Rainier National Park, Washington. Photograph by Mary Liz Austin.

PEACE

Have you ever thought seriously of the meaning of that blessing given to the peacemakers? People are always expecting to get peace in heaven; but you know whatever peace they get there will be ready made. Whatever making of peace *they* can be blest for, must be on the earth here: not the taking of arms against, but the building of nests amidst, its "sea of troubles." Difficult enough, you think? Perhaps so, but I do not see that any of us try. We complain of the want of many things—we want votes, we want liberty, we want amusement, we want money. Which of us feels, or knows, that he wants peace?

There are two ways of getting it, if you don't want it. The first is wholly in your own power; to make ourselves nests of pleasant thoughts. Those are nests on the sea indeed, but safe beyond all others; only they need much art in the building. None of us yet knows what fairy palaces we may build of beautiful thoughts— proof against all adversity. Bright fancies, satisfied memories, noble histories, faithful savings, precious and restful thoughts, which care cannot disturb, nor pain make gloomy—houses built without hands, for our souls to live in.

John Ruskin

GIVE ME PEACE

With eager heart and will on fire,
I strove to win my great desire.
"Peace shall be mine," I said; but life
Grew bitter in the barren strife.

My soul was weary, and my pride
Was wounded deep; to heaven I cried,
"God grant me peace or I must die";
The dumb stars glittered no reply.

Broken at last, I bowed my head,
Forgetting all myself, and said,
"Whatever comes, His will be done";
And in that moment peace was won.

Henry van Dyke

PEACE, LIKE A LAMB

I lie sleepless in the half light,
Seeing through bare trees outside
The gray wolf sky of pallid stars.
I lie alone and wait,
Not for the tap of robin's beak upon the pane,
The unexpected wind that shakes
The icicles along the eaves
And ruffles up the new-dropped snow,
I wait for every earthly sound to die away:
Until from nothingness I slowly hear
Peace, like a lamb, move softly from field to field,
The crunching tread of strangers on the hills,
And unfamiliar voices in the trees,
And then, a waterfall of wings
Taking possession of the startled air.

Leonard Clark

Frozen branches on a cluster of pine trees make a wintry scene in LaSalle County, Illinois. Photograph by Terry Donnelly.

The icy, cold waters of The Big Woods River makes a narrow pathway under a snow covered bridge and

alongside a spectacular tree speckled mountain in Idaho. Photograph by Dick Dietrich Photography.

Barter

Life has loveliness to sell,
All beautiful and splendid things,
Blue waves whitened on a cliff,
Soaring fire that sways and sings
And children's faces looking up
Holding wonder like a cup.

Life has loveliness to sell,
Music like a curve of gold,
Scent of pine trees in the rain,
Eyes that love you, arms that hold,
And for the spirit's still delight,
Holy thoughts that star the night.

Spend all you have for loveliness,
Buy it and never count the cost;
For one white singing hour of peace
Count many a year of strife well lost,
And for a breath of ecstasy
Give all you have been, or could be.

Sara Teasdale

Winter

A sky eiderdown enfolds the lean
And shivering trees; each field and hill
Now wears upon its skeleton a clean
Close-fitting cloak of snow; once noisy rill
Calls softly through its narrowed corridor
Assurance to the life, snow-locked below.
The leaf is gone, the lilting troubadour,
The vivid blooms of Summer's flashing show.
The earth unfolds quintessent purity
Before our very eyes for all to know—
And God, to spare the shrinking soul of me,
Sifts down a veil of softly falling snow.

Sylvia Trent Auxier

Clear Creek Canyon in San Isabel National Forest, Colorado finds itself in the midst of winter. Photograph by Terry Donnelly

Readers' Reflections

MY NEIGHBOR'S LIGHT

My neighbor's light is gleaming
For me across the snow.
When first I see its beaming,
It sets my heart aglow.

I know within the shelter
Of the house across the way,
Someone is up and stirring
Before the dawn of day.

Then later in the morning
I'll hear the merry glee
Of happy childish voices
Come floating out to me.

I can see the aged grandsire
By the window in his chair.
His face lights up with pleasure
As I call to greet him there.

My neighbor's light is gleaming
Like a beacon every morn.
It gives me strength and courage
For the tasks that must be borne.

Behind his shining window
A light of warm affection glows—
O neighbor keep it burning
For me across the snow.

Eunice I. Gardner
Salem, Utah

CHRISTMAS CIRCLES

Gifts for friends and family
Make a circle around our tree.
And on each door new wreaths are seen,
Circles made of evergreen.
On winter nights with friends we share
A round of carols and a prayer
As holding hands we make a ring
Filled with joy as we sing.
Circles of the season's cheer—
It's Christmas rounding out the year.

Ericka Northrop
Tucson, Arizona

LAST DETAIL

It's Christmas Eve and finally
The kids are all in bed,
And milk and cookies are laid out
So Santa can be fed.

The gifts are almost finished,
Just one large toy to do.
I'll wrap it very quickly
Then we'll at last be through.

I lift the box and suddenly
I feel a stab of fear,
For nothing is as chilling
As the message printed here.

I know there'll be no sleep tonight
Even though I am bone tired,
For I've learned to my horror
"Some assembly is required."

Paul Swope
Fort Washington, Maryland

WINTER'S ETCHING

Through my frosted window pane,
I watched with pure delight
As silvery moonlight laced with snow
Slumbered silently through the night.

The north wind blew a soft refrain
As it waltzed across the snow,
Swirling little furrows
With every gentle blow.

Upon the purple shadows
The woodland bunnies played
While cold little sentries marched
In an icicle parade.

And lacy little snowflakes
Gently drifted down
To lay a feathery blanket
Upon the sleeping town.

Roberta Carpenter
Goshen, Indiana

TO CHURCH ON CHRISTMAS EVE

To church on Christmas Eve we go
   With Grandpa's horse and sleigh,
Through the snow with stars above
   To guide us on our way.

All bundled up against the cold,
   Hot bricks beneath our feet
As we dream of Christmas Eve at church
   And the birth of Christ, so sweet.

Everything is dressed in white
   As we travel down the road,
So full of joy and love for all
   We feel we could explode.

So fresh and clean and crisp the air
   On this special night of nights,

While up ahead we see the church
   All lit with welcoming lights.

Inside with friends and neighbors dear
   We worship the newborn King,
Lifting voices up to Him
   As carols in praise we sing.

The bells ring out at midnight
   From the church on Christmas Eve,
Proclaiming peace on earth to all
   As we prepare to leave,

Taking with us hope and love
   As we climb back in the sleigh,
Remembering that Christ is why
   We have a Christmas Day.

Sandra Chance
Westville, Indiana

Editor's Note: Readers are invited to submit unpublished, original poetry for possible publica-
tion in future issues of Ideals. Please send typed copies only; manuscripts will not be returned.
Writers receive $10 for each published submission. Send material to Readers' Reflections,
Ideals Publications Inc., P.O. Box 305300, Nashville, Tennessee 37230-5300.

A male evening grosbeak rests a moment in his search for food. Photograph by Superstock.

WINTER BLOSSOMS

My garden dreams beneath
A fleecy coverlet,
But sparrows frisking there
Seem small brown mignonette.
Blue jays remind my heart
Of bluebells in the spring.

And cardinals become
Red roses on the wing.
With deep delight I watch
These blossoms in the snow.
And now and then I boast
A rare black tulip crow.

Gail Brook Burket

A male bluejay finds some juicy berries in the snowy landscape. Photograph by Gay Bumgarner.

SNOW IN THE NIGHT

The snow came tumbling from the sky,
The noisy wind was blustery,
It whirled the flakes in spiral sheets
And etched bare trees with filigree.
The houses looked like frosted cakes
With icing dripping from their eaves,
And little shrubs stood wistfully
With heaping spoonfuls on their leaves.
And then the wind was very still,
And, waiting for the world to wake,
It gazed at dawn with awe upon
The fairyland it helped to make.

Isla Paschal Richardson

From My Garden Journal
by Deana Deck

INDOOR CITRUS TREES

One of the memories I carry with me from childhood is the unforgettable fragrance of orange blossoms, which I discovered on my first trip to Florida. During World War II, my father, an army captain, frequently had to transfer from one side of the continent to another. One year, around Christmastime, my father learned that he would be transferring to a unit in Florida. After we all celebrated Christmas together at my grandparents' home in Oklahoma, my father left early and drove to Florida to report to his new unit and to find a place for us to live. My mother followed him by train a few weeks later with two preschoolers (myself included) in tow. As the train pulled in to Gainesville, we opened the windows to seek a glimpse of our father. Suddenly, the heady aroma of orange blossoms enveloped us, and we realized that the train was making its way through orange orchards in the full bloom of mid-winter. At the age of four, I was marked for life with the unforgettable fra-

grance of orange blossoms.

The orange and its fragrant blossom have a long history. Oranges originated in China and made their way to the Mediterranean and the Middle East. The Arabians and Persians called the fruit *naranj*, from which the name *orange* evolved. The Greeks believed the orange to be the exclusive property of the gods on Mt. Olympus, who jealously guarded their precious commodity against theft by mere mortals. The Romans thought the orange tree resembled the cedar; thus, they called the fruit *citrus sinensis*, which translates into "Chinese cedar apple." The Romans also considered the orange to be a symbol of love, and to this day, orange blossoms are associated with weddings. Much later, during the Age of Exploration, the orange came to the Americas with Columbus, and the fruit quickly adapted and began to thrive in the humid tropical areas of the New World, including the area that would become Florida.

You too can enjoy the fragrance and beauty of the orange, and you do not need to travel to the sunshine state. You can grow orange plants in your own home, in just about any part of the country. You will find mature container-grown citrus plants at most garden centers. The most commonly available plants are the Meyer lemon (*Citrus limon*) and the Mandarin lime (*Citrus x limonia*), both of which bear fruit in all stages of development and make attractive holiday decorations. The blossoms are as fragrant as those found on field-grown trees, but the fruit, though edible, is on the bitter side. Do not plan on making your own orange juice from these acrid little fruits.

Whereas nursery-grown plants are more reliable, it is also fun to start your own plants from seed. All you need is a pot, some sandy soil, and a few orange seeds. For that matter, you can use the seeds of any citrus fruit you prefer. The different seeds are all equally easy to grow in containers. Before you start, however, you must learn more about the nature of each plant.

First, you need to be flexible about what type of plant you want. There are practically no pure strains of any citrus species sold in supermarkets today. All oranges, lemons, tangerines, and grapefruits are hybrids bred to produce tasty fruit that is disease-resistant in the field, ships well, and has a long shelf life. Therefore, if you save a seed from the orange you ate for breakfast, it will germinate and produce a plant that resembles one of its parents, but it is impossible to predict the plant's dominant characteristics. In the case of the orange, you can hedge your bets by deciding between the thin-skinned Florida orange, which produces more juice, and the California orange, which has a thick skin and a meatier fruit that is more suitable for eating out of hand.

It is also important to be aware that the flavor of the fruit on your indoor citrus tree will be significantly more sour than store-bought oranges. Still, indoor oranges are great for making marmalade, they look beautiful on the plant, and they smell just as wonderful as if they had been grown in an orchard.

Finally, you need to be patient with your citrus plant. In nature, a citrus tree can take up to ten years to mature enough to blossom and produce fruit. If your plant suffers from a lack of light or humidity or poor pollination, it may never produce much in the way of blossoms or fruit. You can, however, still reap the benefit of its fragrance. The shiny green leaves of all citrus plants are highly fragrant and, even as young seedlings, they bring a tangy fresh scent to any room. The citrus leaves blend especially well with the aroma of a Christmas tree; as a result, they make an excellent base for a spicy potpourri, which you can give to friends as a Christmas gift.

Now that you know the benefits of growing citrus plants, you should learn *how* to grow them. First, fill a ten-inch terra cotta pot with rich soil; add a couple of cups of clean, salt-free sand to aid drainage and mix well. Then plant each seed about one-half inch deep in the soil. Place your plant in an area of your home that receives plenty of light. Direct sunlight is preferable, for which a greenhouse is divine, but a couple of grow-lights or even a 100-watt light bulb will persuade a potted citrus plant to grow in a dim apartment.

Citrus plants are also known to thrive in the vicinity of the sea. To keep your plant happy, it is wise to reproduce these conditions as much as possible. In a centrally-heated home in the winter, the plant will require frequent misting to provide the humidity it craves. Your plant also will require thorough waterings with tepid water. Allow the soil to dry slightly between waterings; if the top inch or so of the soil is dry, it is time to water. The plant will let you know how you are doing; its leaves will wilt if the soil is too wet or too dry.

Once your plant has begun to grow, you will need to decide whether you want to keep it indoors year-round or move it outside in the summer. Mature citrus trees range from eight to twenty feet in height, and they must be kept pot-bound if they are to spend their winters indoors and summers on the patio. You can keep the plant healthy by resisting the urge to repot it in a larger pot and also by carefully pruning the top to keep its proportions manageable.

It may seem like an indoor citrus plant needs a lot of attention, but the first time you brush against its fragrant foliage or catch the scent of a newly opened blossom wafting through the air, you will realize why the Greeks revered the orange as a treasure of the gods.

Deana Deck tends her flowers, plants, and vegetables at her home in Nashville, Tennessee, where her popular garden column is a regular feature in The Tennessean.

Velvet Shoes

Let us walk in the white snow
In a soundless space;
With footsteps quiet and slow,
At a tranquil pace,
Under veils of white lace.
I shall go shod in silk,
And you in wool,
White as a white cow's milk,
More beautiful
Than the breast of a gull.

We shall walk through the still town
In a windless peace;
We shall step upon white down,
Upon silver fleece,
Upon softer than these.

We shall walk in velvet shoes:
Wherever we go
Silence will fall like dews
On white silence below.
We shall walk in the snow.

Elinor Wylie

*American artist Donald Zolan shares his vision of a little girl exploring her world
in Winter Wonder. © Zolan Fine Arts, Ltd., Hershey, Pennsylvania.*

a Bell

Had I the power
To cast a bell that should
     from some great tower,
At the first Christmas hour,
Out-ring,
And fling
A jubilant message wide,
The forgéd metals should be thus allied;
No iron Pride,
But soft Humility and rich-veined Hope
Cleft from a sunny slope,
And there should be
White Charity,
And silvery Love that knows not
     Doubt nor Fear,
To make the peal more clear;
And then, to firmly fix the fine alloy,
There should be joy!

Clinton Scollard

Freshly fallen snow covers a meeting house in Canaan, New Hampshire. Photograph by William Johnson/Johnson's Photography.

Bits & Pieces

The time draws near the birth of Christ:
The moon is hid; the night is still;
The Christmas bells from hill to hill
Answer each other in the mist.

    Alfred, Lord Tennyson

Ring out, ye crystal spheres,
Once, bless our human ears,
(If ye have power to touch our senses so:)
And let your silver chime
Move in melodious time,
And let the bass of heaven's deep organ blow,
And with your ninefold harmony
Make up full consort to the angelic symphony.

    John Milton

I heard the bells on Christmas Day
Their old, familiar carols play
And wild and sweet
The words repeat
Of peace on earth, good-will to men!

    Henry Longfellow

How soft the music of those village bells,
Falling at intervals upon the ear
In cadence sweet.

    William Cowper

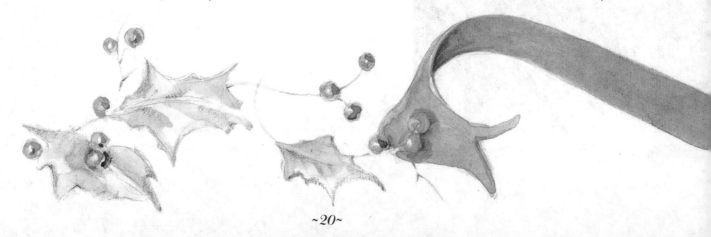

Let's dance and sing and make good cheer,
For Christmas comes but once a year.

G. MacFerran

We rejoice in the light,
And we echo the song
That comes down through the night
From the heavenly throng.
Ay! we shout to the lovely evangel they bring,
And we greet in His cradle our Saviour and King.

Josiah Gilbert Holland

Oh, surely melody from heaven was sent
To cheer the soul when tired with human strife,
To soothe the wayward heart by sorrow rent,
And soften down the rugged road of life!

Henry Kirke White

Ring out the old, ring in the new,
Ring, happy bells, across the snow:
The year is going, let him go;
Ring out the false, ring in the true.

Alfred, Lord Tennyson

THAT CHRISTMAS LONG AGO

Above a lowly stable dim
A star shone wondrous bright
To herald the birth of a King
Born on that holy night.

He wore no royal diadem,
Nor palace did He claim.
But oh, He truly was a king;
Messiah was His name.

Awe-struck shepherds came and knelt,
The wee king to adore;
The magi brought their royal gifts,
Star-led to stable door.

And in that hallowed cattle shed,
All was love and light
As angels hovered round the Babe,
A truly wondrous sight.

Love came down from heaven
And ever set man's heart aglow
When Christ was born in Bethlehem
That Christmas long ago.

Kay Hoffman

PRAYER

Last night I crept across the snow,
Where only tracking rabbits go,
And then I waited quite alone
Until the Christmas radiance shone.

At midnight twenty angels came,
Each white and shining like a flame.
At midnight twenty angels sang,
The stars swung out like bells and rang.

They lifted me across the hill,
They bore me in their arms until
A greater glory greeted them.
It was the town of Bethlehem.

And gently, then, they set me down,
All worshipping that holy town,

And gently, then, they bade me raise
My head to worship and to praise.

And gently, then, the Christ smiled down.
Ah, there was glory in that town!
It was as if the world were free
And glistening with purity.

And in that vault of crystal blue,
It was as if the world were new,
And myriad angels, file on file,
Gloried in the Christ-child's smile.

It was so beautiful to see
Such glory, for a child like me,
So beautiful, it does not seem
It could have been a Christmas dream.

John Farrar

SHEPHERDS, SIT WE HERE

Sweet music, sweeter far
Than any song is sweet;
Sweet music, heavenly rare,
Mine ears (O peers!) doth greet.
You gentle flocks, whose fleeces, pearl'd with dew,
Resemble heaven, whom golden drops make bright,
Listen, O listen! now, O not to you
Our pipes make sport to shorten weary night.
But voices most divine,
Make blissful harmony;
Voices that seem to shine,
For what else clears the sky?
Tunes can we hear, but not the singers see:
The tunes divine, and so the singers be.

Lo! how the firmament
Within as azure fold
The flock of stars hath pent,
That we might them behold.
Yet from their beams proceedeth not this light,
Nor can their crystals such reflection give.
What, then, doth make the element so bright?
The heavens are come down upon the earth live.
But hearken to the song:
'Glory to glory's King!
And peace all men among!'
These choristers do sing.
Angels they are, as also, shepherds, he
Whom in our fear we do admire to see.

'Let not amazement blind
Your souls,' said he, 'annoy;
To you and all mankind,
My message bringeth joy.
For, lo! the world's great Shepherd now is born,
A blesséd babe, an infant full of power;
After long night uprisen is the morn,
Renowning Bethlehem in the Saviour.
Sprung is the perfect day,
By prophets seen afar;
Sprung is the mirthful May,
Which Winter cannot mar.'
In David's city doth this sun appear,
Clouded in flesh, yet, shepherds, sit we here?

Edmund Bolton

Ornaments and lace adorn the sheet music of famous Christmas carols. Photograph by Nancy Matthews.

This Most Special Night

Soft is the sound of a donkey's hoofed feet
As slowly it's led down a Bethlehem street.
For the burden it bears is a young, pregnant wife
Who carries within her the glorious life
Of a Child to be born this most special night,
And a great star is casting its radiant light
To brighten their way to a neighboring inn
Where the voices of guests can be heard from within.

But the innkeeper says he must turn them away,
Suggesting a stable as a place they can stay.
So Mary and Joseph wait there in the gloom

German artist Robert Leinweber captures the warmth of the Christmas scene, Adoration of the Shepherds. Superstock.

Till Jesus is born in this cold, rustic room
And laid in a manger, surrounded by sheep
Who are puzzled, no doubt, by the company they keep;
And it seems such a poor, inappropriate thing—
This manger that cradles a newly born King.

Yet tonight the whole earth becomes His birthplace;
For the billowing seas foam to pillows of lace,
The valleys and meadows His cradle enfold,
And the hillsides form coverlets, emerald and gold.
The murmuring streams send Him sweet lullabies,
And His robes are white clouds and the blue velvet skies;
While the angels rejoice in the heavens above
As the Father smiles down on His Son with love!

John Bonser

THROUGH MY WINDOW

Pamela Kennedy

Art by Russ Flint

CHRISTMAS ANGEL

Celestin knew the time was nearing. Not because time mattered to him, but because it was important to Majesty. When the fullness of time arrived, Celestin wanted to be ready to obey instantly. Obedience was the highest service among the angels. It was their never-ending gift to Majesty.

Celestin often pondered the way obedience seemed so difficult for humans. He didn't understand that. Limited as they were by time and space, it seemed only logical that they would want to experience life on earth to the fullest. After all, their days were brief. Couldn't they see that Majesty knew best? He spoke His eternal wisdom to them in nature, whispered it to them through their souls, wrote it in His Word, and shouted it through His prophets. Still they resisted. Now, in an act of grace and mercy Celestin couldn't comprehend, Majesty was sending the Only Begotten to these stiff-necked creatures. Surely now, they would finally learn obedience and experience the richness of living according to their Maker's will.

It had been almost a year in earth time since Gabriel traveled to Nazareth to speak to Mary. Celestin understood why she had been chosen. He had watched as Gabriel told the young maiden of Majesty's plan. Despite her troubled questions, she had bowed her head in humble obedience and said, "I am the Lord's servant. May it be to me as you have said." Oh, how the angelic choir had rejoiced at that moment! Celestin could still hear the chords of praise echoing in the eternal reaches of heaven.

Celestin wondered how Majesty would introduce the Only Begotten to the world. Perhaps it would be in a mighty temple with row upon row of priests praising God and blowing trumpets. Maybe there would be a tremendous earthquake or tidal wave presaging the event. Majesty used pillars of fire and parted water when he helped Moses, but Celestin felt sure there would be something more magnificent and wonderful for the Only Begotten. He would have to wait and see. Impatience was not becoming of an angel.

When the call came it was not at all what Celestin had expected. He was to take a multitude of angels and travel to a dark hillside outside a little town called Bethlehem. There he was to make an announcement to a small group of poor men tending a flock of sheep. He was to say: "Do not be afraid. I bring you good news of great joy that will be for all people. Today in the town of David a Saviour has been born to you; he is Christ the Lord. This will be a sign to you; you will find a baby wrapped in cloths and lying in a manger." At that point, he was to lead his fellow angels in choruses of praise to God.

"Are you sure that's it?" Celestin asked the messenger from the Throne. "No temple or palace or parted seas or comet shower or anything?"

The other angel shook his head. Then he raised his hand as if remembering something. "Oh, there will be a star," he added.

"A star?" Celestin repeated incredulously. "Just one star?"

"Yes," the messenger repeated with a sigh, "just one star—over a little animal shelter, behind an inn, on a back alley in Bethlehem."

"With all due respect," Celestin continued, "do you think you could have misunderstood the message? We're talking about the Only Begotten here, the Creator, the Sustainer, the Holy One."

The other angel squared his shoulders and looked just a bit perturbed. "That is the message as Majesty gave it to me. I do not question Him." He vanished, leaving Celestin alone and stinging from the mild rebuke.

"Well, I only asked," he muttered. "I wasn't planning to disobey!"

Quickly he summoned a company of angels and led them to the assigned hillside. The shepherds fell on the ground and quaked, just as Celestin had known they would. Humans were always so discom-

fited by the sight of angels. He reassured them then with Majesty's words and led the angelic choir as they sang, "Glory to God in the highest, and on earth peace to men." He would have preferred something with more hallelujahs, but that wasn't in the orders for tonight.

When the angelic chorus ended and the others returned to heaven, Celestin remained behind. He wanted to see the Only Begotten. He still could not fathom why Majesty had chosen such a homely way to introduce such magnificence.

Silently Celestin hovered in the shadows of the tiny stable. The silver light of one pure star softly illuminated the stony walls. Mary, the obedient one, and Joseph, her loving husband, reclined on the straw. In her arms she held an infant wrapped in swaddling cloths. Could this be the Only Begotten—here, in these rude surroundings? It was unthinkable. Celestin recalled the dazzling light originating from Majesty's throne, the myriad angels constantly in attendance, the never-ending praises attending His presence. And then he gazed once more at the little family surrounded only by sleeping cows and sheep.

Suddenly, a solitary word flashed into Celestin's mind with brilliant clarity: *love*. Here in this humble setting Majesty had spoken it not with thunder or earthquake, nor with an angelic chorus or even a single trumpet blast, but with flesh and blood. The Only Begotten had left the glories of heaven to bring true love to humanity. Here in this tiny town it would begin, but Celestin knew such love could never be confined. Time or space, even eternity, would not be sufficient to contain such abundance. It would flow like a river watering the souls of generation after generation of earth's citizens. A twinge of envy touched Celestin's heart as he realized even an angel could never know such joy as this. He bowed then in reverence before the tiny one lying in Mary's arms, and a gentle breeze brushed the Baby's cheek as the angel whispered, "Holy, Holy, Holy."

Pamela Kennedy is a freelance writer of short stories, articles, essays, and children's books. Wife of a retired naval officer and mother of three children, she has made her home on both U.S. coasts and currently resides in Honolulu, Hawaii.

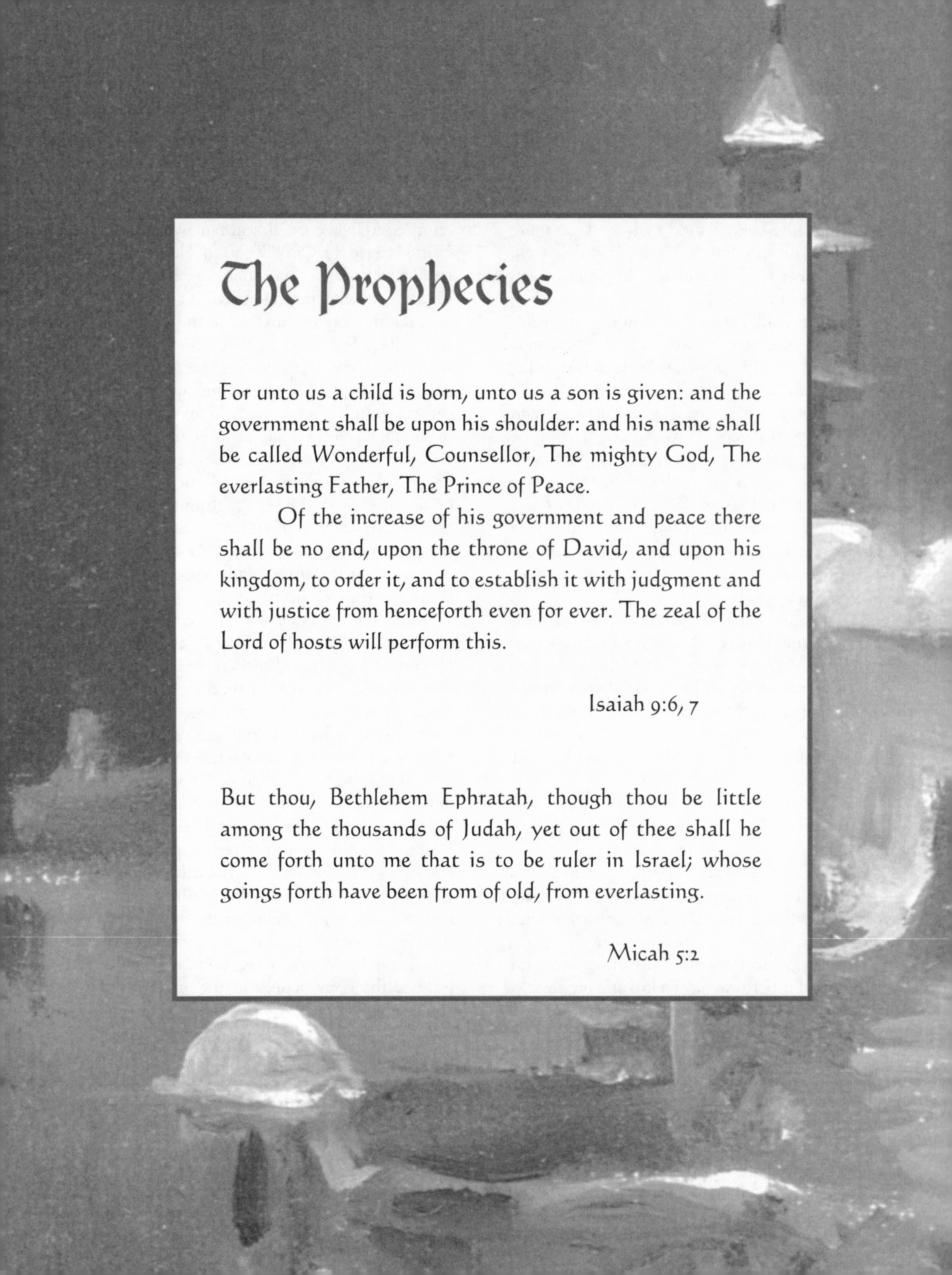

The Prophecies

For unto us a child is born, unto us a son is given: and the government shall be upon his shoulder: and his name shall be called Wonderful, Counsellor, The mighty God, The everlasting Father, The Prince of Peace.

Of the increase of his government and peace there shall be no end, upon the throne of David, and upon his kingdom, to order it, and to establish it with judgment and with justice from henceforth even for ever. The zeal of the Lord of hosts will perform this.

Isaiah 9:6, 7

But thou, Bethlehem Ephratah, though thou be little among the thousands of Judah, yet out of thee shall he come forth unto me that is to be ruler in Israel; whose goings forth have been from of old, from everlasting.

Micah 5:2

Then shall we know, if we follow on to know the Lord: his going forth is prepared as the morning; and he shall come unto us as the rain, as the latter and former rain unto the earth.

Hosea 6:3

And there shall come forth a rod out of the stem of Jesse, and a Branch shall grow out of his roots: And the spirit of the Lord shall rest upon him, the spirit of wisdom and understanding, the spirit of counsel and might, the spirit of knowledge and of the fear of the Lord;

And shall make him of quick understanding in the fear of the Lord. . . . And righteousness shall be the girdle of his loins, and faithfulness the girdle of his reins. The wolf also shall dwell with the lamb, and the leopard shall lie down with the kid; and the calf and the young lion and the fatling together; and a little child shall lead them.

Isaiah 11: 1–3, 5, 6

The Nativity

And it came to pass in those days, that there went out a decree from Caesar Augustus, that all the world should be taxed. (And this taxing was first made when Cyrenius was governor of Syria.)

And all went to be taxed, every one into his own city. And Joseph also went up from Galilee, out of the city of Nazareth, into Judaea, unto the city of David, which is called Bethlehem; (because he was of the house and lineage of David:)

To be taxed with Mary his espoused wife, being great with child. And so it was, that, while they were there, the days were accomplished that she should be delivered.

And she brought forth her firstborn son, and wrapped him in a swaddling clothes, and laid him in a manger; because there was no room for them in the inn.

Luke 2:1-7

The Annunciation to the Shepherds

And there were in the same country shepherds abiding in the field, keeping watch over their flock by night. And, lo, the angel of the Lord came upon them, and the glory of the Lord shone round about them: and they were sore afraid.

And the angel said unto them, Fear not: for, behold, I bring you good tidings of great joy, which shall be to all people. For unto you is born this day in the city of David a Saviour, which is Christ the Lord. And this shall be a sign unto you; Ye shall find the babe wrapped in swaddling clothes, lying in a manger.

And suddenly there was with the angel a multitude of the heavenly host praising God, and saying, Glory to God in the highest, and on earth peace, good will toward men. And it came to pass, as the angels were gone away from them into heaven, the shepherds said one to another, Let us now go even unto Bethlehem, and see this thing which is come to pass, which the Lord hath made known unto us. And they came with haste, and found Mary, and Joseph, and the babe lying in a manger.

Luke 2:8–16

The Adoration of the Magi

Now when Jesus was born in Bethlehem of Judaea in the days of Herod the king, behold, there came wise men from the east to Jerusalem, Saying, Where is he that is born King of the Jews? for we have seen his star in the east, and are come to worship him.

Then Herod, when he had privily called the wise men, inquired of them diligently what time the star appeared. And he sent them to Bethlehem, and said, Go and search diligently for the young child; and when ye have found him, bring me word again, that I may come and worship him also. When they had heard the king, they departed; and, lo, the star, which they saw in the east, went before them, till it came and stood over where the young child was. When they saw the star, they rejoiced with exceeding great joy. And when they were come into the house, they saw the young child with Mary his mother, and fell down, and worshipped him: and when they had opened their treasures, they presented unto him gifts; gold, and frankincense, and myrrh.

Matthew 2:1–2, 7–11

The Flight

And when they were departed, behold, the angel of the Lord appeareth to Joseph in a dream, saying, Arise, and take the young child and his mother, and flee into Egypt, and be thou there until I bring thee word: for Herod will seek the young child to destroy him.

When he arose, he took the young child and his mother by night, and departed into Egypt: And was there until the death of Herod: that it might be fulfilled which was spoken of the Lord by the prophet, saying, Out of Egypt have I called my son.

Matthew 2:13–15

Devotions FROM THE Heart

Pamela Kennedy

"Saying, Where is he that is born King of the Jews?
for we have seen his star in the east, and are come to worship him."
Matthew 2:2

SEEKING, FOLLOWING, LISTENING

When the Magi left the security of their Persian homeland to look for the answer to their prayers, it was with the faith of diligent seekers. They were wise men who recognized there was more to truth than what they knew. When the mystical star appeared on the horizon, they packed their bags and followed it even though they were unsure of their destination. This is the way with all good seekers; they begin from where they are, using the revelation available at the time, and head out, confident that along the way their destination will be made plain. So many of us fear to start along the path of discovery because we cannot see the end clearly. True wisdom understands the importance of just beginning, the importance of being a seeker.

Arriving in Jerusalem, the Magi discovered they were in the wrong place. There was no king of the Jews in residence there and no one seemed to know of his existence. But as they persisted in their inquiry, they received direction. It might have been tempting to give up at this point, to turn back, to doubt their initial faith in the star. But they chose instead to follow the guidance of King Herod and his counselors even though it seemed unusual. They left the temples and courts of Jerusalem and headed for a little hamlet called Bethlehem.

Like these seekers, we sometimes arrive at blind alleys and wrong turns on our search for truth. The path which seemed so clear when we started out instead leads to disappointment. That is often the time to open our hearts and minds to a different path, to follow a new direction. When the Magi did this they discovered what they thought they had missed. There in an unexpected corner of an unremarkable town, they found the answer to their prayers. They found the Christ.

With their search ended and their goal attained, the Wise Men might have supposed they had nothing more to learn. They would have been wrong. For in the stillness following the joy at the end of their journey, God spoke and led them in a new direction, warning them to return home another way. Had they been unwilling to listen, content in the achievement of their own goals, they might have missed the vital word of truth.

As seekers we also may be tempted to feel our journey is ended when our prayers are answered. But this is the time when we must carefully listen. Often God grants our desires not only so we may find joy and fulfillment, but so we may also hear His voice leading us in new and different paths.

This Christmas season let us follow the wise example of the Magi. Seek God with diligence, follow as He gives us insights and direction along the way, and listen as He guides us on beyond our expectations to new areas of growth and service.

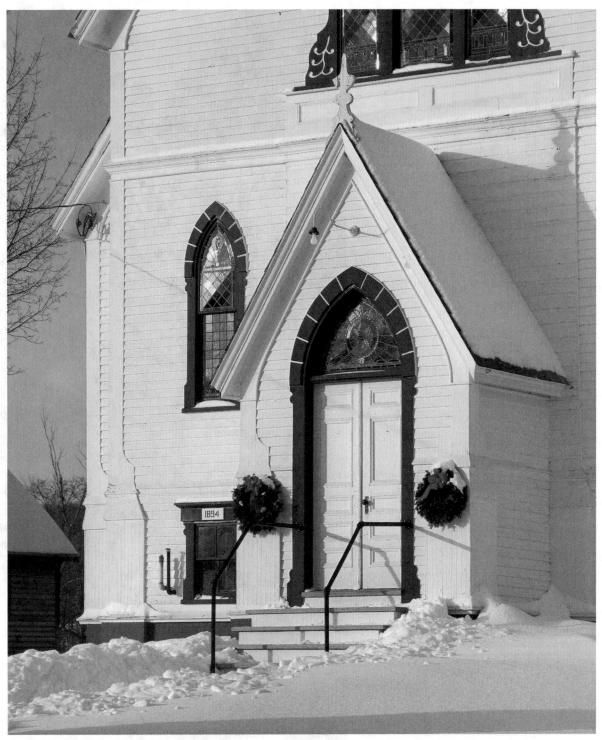

A church in Ryegate Corner, Vermont captures the spirit of Christmas. Photograph by William Johnson/Johnson's Photography

Prayer: Dear God who led the wise men of old,
please guide and direct my path each day as I
seek to hear and follow Your voice. Amen.

A MOTHER'S REFLECTION

Sweet little Babe in bed of straw,
Upon thy face I gaze with awe.
You truly are God's own dear Son,
Messiah, the long awaited one.

The shepherds come, Thee to adore
And humbly kneel on straw-strewn floor;
Magi, star-led o'er desert sand,
Have brought Thee jewels from a far land.

The oxen gaze with wondering eyes;
To them You are a sweet surprise.
Gentle doves draw near to coo
Their own soft lullaby to You.

A poor young maid—the chosen one
To be the mother of God's Son?
To me it seemed a strange request—
Among all women I'm most blessed.

My tiny Babe in bed of straw,
You are the Saviour born for all.
God's gift of love sent from on high—
Sleep little one till dawn draws nigh.
The whole world will Thy birth recall,
Messiah born in a stable stall.

Kay Hoffman

Old fashioned toys and a vase full of Christmas foliage bring cheer to the holiday season. Photograph by Nancy Matthews.

A CRADLE SONG

Sweet dreams, form a shade
O'er my lovely infant's head;
Sweet dreams of pleasant streams
By happy, silent, moony beams.
Sweet sleep, with soft down
Weave thy brows an infant crown.
Sweet sleep, Angel mild,
Hover o'er my happy child.
Sweet smiles, in the night
Hover over my delight;
Sweet smiles, mother's smiles,
All the livelong night beguiles.
Sweet moans, dove-like sighs,
Chase not slumber from the eyes.
Sweets moans, sweeter smiles,
All the dove-like moans beguiles.
Sleep, sleep, happy child,
All creation slept and smil'd;
Sleep, sleep, happy sleep,
While o'er thee thy mother weep.
Sweet babe, in thy
Holy image I can trace.
Sweet babe once like thee,
Thy Maker lay and wept for me,
Wept for me, for thee, for all,
When He was an infant small.
Thou His image ever see,
Heavenly face that smiles on thee,
Smiles on thee, on me, on all;
Who became an infant small.
Infant smiles are His own smiles;
Heaven and earth to peace beguiles

William Blake

Christmas Once Is Christmas Still

The silent skies are full of speech
For who hath ears to hear;
The winds are whispering each to each,
The moon is calling to the beech,
And stars their sacred mission teach,
Of Faith, and Love, and Fear.

But once the sky its silence broke,
And song o'erflowed the earth,
The midnight air with glory shook,
And angels mortal language spoke,
When God our human nature took,
In Christ the Saviour's birth.

And Christmas once is Christmas still;
The gates through which He came,
And forests wild and murmuring rill,
And fruitful field and breezy hill,
And all that else the wide world fill,
Are vocal with His name.

Shall we not listen while they sing,
This latest Christmas morn,
And music hear in everything,
And faithful lives in tribute bring
To the great song which greets the King
Who comes when Christ is born?

The sky can still remember
The earliest Christmas morn,
When in the cold December
The Saviour Christ was born;

And still in darkness clouded,
And still in noonday light,
It feels its far depths crowded
With angels fair and bright.

O never failing splendor!
O never silent song!
Still keep the green earth tender,
Still keep the gray earth strong;
Still keep the brave earth dreaming
Of deeds that shall be done,
While children's lives come streaming
Like sunbeams from the sun.

No stars unfold its glory,
No trumpet's wind is blown,
But tells the Christmas story
In music of its own.
No eager strife of mortals,
In busy fields or town,
But sees the open portals
Through which the Christ came down.

O Angels sweet and splendid,
Throng in our hearts, and sing
The wonders which attended
The coming of the King;
Till we, too, boldly pressing
Where once the Angel trod,
Climb Bethlehem's Hill of Blessing,
And find the Son of God.

Phillips Brooks

The snow capped peaks of the Grand Tetons welcome a new day. Photograph by Terry Donnelly.

A village in Stark, New Hampshire, sparkles on a winter night.

SNOWFLAKES

And did you know
That every flake of snow
That forms so high
In the gray winter sky
And falls so far
Is a bright six-pointed star?
Each crystal grows
A flower as perfect as a rose.
Lace could never make
The patterns of a flake.
No brooch
Of figured silver could approach
Its delicate craftsmanship. And think:

Each pattern is distinct.
Of all the snowflakes floating there—
The million million in the air—
None is the same. Each star
Is newly forged, as faces are,
Shaped to its own design
Like yours and mine.
And yet . . . each one
Melts when its flight is done;
Holds frozen loveliness
A moment, even less;
Suspends itself in time—
And passes like a rhyme.

Clive Sansom

WINTER NIGHT

Pile high the hickory and the light
Log of chestnut struck by the blight.
Welcome in the winter night.

The day has gone in hewing and felling,
Sawing and drawing wood to the dwelling
For the night of talk and story-telling.

These are the hours that give the edge
To the blunted axe and the bent wedge,
Straighten the saw and lighten the sledge.

Here are the question and reply,
And the fire reflected in the thinking eye.
So peace, and let the bob-cat cry.

Edna St. Vincent Millay

China dolls wait under the Christmas tree to surprise their new owners. Photograph by Jessie Walker.

Christmas Shopping

I came upon her suddenly as she, in placid reverie,
Sat gazing on the hurrying crowd outside the windows of a shop
Bedecked in glistening holly wreaths.
Long golden curls and eyes of china blue.
My eyes met hers and smiled.
So many years have dolls and I conspired on Christmas Eve,
And this one, just the size for little arms . . .
(I see a dimpled hand upraised lest I
Awake the doll that's being rocked to sleep.)
The crowd is jostling me, and I, remembering,
Retrace my steps.
It was the shop next door I wanted—
"Sporting Goods"—that's it . . .
(And now I see a tall slim form,
The lithe, athletic lankness of a growing girl
Whose sparkling eyes laugh in life's face.) . . . Oh, yes,
A tennis racket—that was on my list.
But entering, I cast a backward, wistful glance
Where gaze blue china eyes
Serene and smiling on a hurrying world,
Serene—as if they did not know
That childhood is the fleeting thing it is—
Gone all too soon!

Isla Paschal Richardson

The Toy Cupboard

Look into the cupboard where the broken toys are put—
The engine with a missing wheel, the doll without a foot—
The storybook no longer read, the fairy with no wings.
Surely something could be done with these discarded things.

Couldn't they be mended well enough to give away?
Empty stocking they would help to fill for Christmas Day.
Brush that shabby teddy, paint the bricks, and clean the swan.
Bring the old toys back to life. Don't keep them. Pass them on.

Patience Strong

Antique toys await new owners to discover them Christmas morning. Photograph by Jessie Walker.

The Parable of the Shopper

My feet were tired, my hands cold, my arms exhausted from the weight of the packages, and it was beginning to snow. The bus was late. I kept rearranging my packages, trying to hold them in a different way in order to give my poor arms a rest.

I still remember that day as if it were yesterday, and yet fifteen years have gone by. Nevertheless, when Christmas rolls around, I remember that day on the bus.

Like I said, I was tired. I had been Christmas shopping all day long. When the bus finally arrived, it was packed with holiday shoppers in the same exhausted mood as I. I sank into the only vacant place, near the back, by a very handsome gentleman. He politely helped me to situate my packages and even held some of them himself.

"My goodness," he said, "did you leave any merchandise still in the stores for the rest of us?"

"I don't think so," I moaned. "Worst of all, I still haven't made all of my purchases."

The woman in the seat behind us joined in my grief and added, "No, the worst thing is that the day after Christmas we will be carrying this same armload back to the store to exchange it."

Her comment brought a general chuckle from all those within earshot, including my seat mate. As the laughter subsided, he began in a quiet, melodious voice, deepened with experience, to teach me a lesson that I have never forgotten.

"Hear now the parable of the shopper," he said, speaking gently and indicating my packages. "A woman went forth to shop, and as she shopped, she carefully planned. Each child's desires were considered. The hard-earned money was divided, and the many purchases were made with the pure joy and delight that is known only to the giver. Then the gifts were wrapped and placed lovingly under the tree.

"In eager anticipation she scanned each face as the gifts were opened.

"'What a lovely sweater,' said the eldest daughter, 'but I think I would prefer blue. I suppose I can exchange it?'

"'Thank you for the cassette player, Mother. It's just what I've always wanted,' said her son. And then aside, secretly to his sister, he continued. 'I told her I wanted the one with the automatic reverse and an extra speaker. I never get what I want!'

"The youngest child spoke out with the spoiled honesty of her age, 'I hate rag dolls! I wanted a china doll. I won't play with it!' And the doll, still in the box, was kicked under the couch.

"One gift still lay under the tree. The woman pointed it out to her husband. 'Your gift is still there.'

"'I'll open it when I have time,' he stated. 'I want to get this bike put together first.'

"How sad it is," continued his soft, beautiful voice. "When gifts are not received in the same spirit they are given. To reject a thoughtful gift is to reject the loving sentiment of the giver himself. And yet, are we not all sometimes guilty of rejecting?"

He was not talking not only to me, but to all of those on the bus. They had all gathered around. The bus was parked.

He took a present from my stack.

"This one," he said, holding it up and pretending to open the card, "could be to you."

He pointed to a rough-looking, teenage boy in a worn denim jacket and pretended to read the gift card.

"'To you I give My life, lived perfectly, as an example so that you might see the pattern and live worthy to return and live with Me again.

Merry Christmas from the Messiah.'

"The gift of example is a precious yet often rejected gift." He set the present down and took another one from my pile.

"This one," he said, holding up a pure, white present, "is for you." He held out the gift to a worn-looking woman, who in earlier years must have been a real beauty and was still attractive in her slim black skirt, black tights, and heels. She read the card out loud and allowed her tears to slip without shame down her painted face.

"'My gift to you is repentance. This Christmas I wish you to know for certain that though your sins be as scarlet, they shall be white as snow, and I the Lord will remember them no more. Have a happy New Year. Signed, your Advocate with the Father.'"

"Ah, repentance, something every Christian needs," said my seat mate.

"But that isn't all. No, here is a big, red package." He looked around the group and brought a ragged, unkempt, little child forward. "This big, red package would be for you if He were here. The card would say, 'On this Christmas and always, My gift to you is love. My love is pure! It is not dependent on what you do or what you look like. I love you as you have been, as you are now, and as you will be in the future. From your brother, Jesus.'"

Then he gently wiped the runny, dirty, upturned nose with his white handkerchief and drew the child into a tight hug.

"And this silver package to you, madam," he said with a bow and handed the gift over to an aging grandmother two rows behind.

"Yes, it would be for you, because you would appreciate it most of the time. His precious gift to you would be the gift of salvation. The surety that you will rise from the grave and live again with a perfect, resurrected body. The card would read, 'I give this precious gift freely to you and all men, by laying down My life for you. Signed, your Saviour.'

"One final gift," said my seat mate. "The greatest of all the gifts of God. Eternal life! A chance to receive the same quality of life that Christ Himself lives. But though this gift is to all men, it must be assembled. He has given us the instructions. They are here in the scriptures." He tore off the paper to reveal a worn, well-used book. "He even has a toll-free number if you need help; anytime, day or night, just pray."

He held our minds and our hearts. We were a hungry audience. Though our shopping had left us drained, now we were being filled by his words.

"How we receive these gifts, these precious gifts from the Babe of Bethlehem, is the telling point. Are we exchangers?" he asked. "Is there really anything else we would rather have?" He searched our eyes and our souls. "Is there a feature missing? It is what we do with a gift long after we have opened it that shows our true appreciation. Have we used it, worn it, displayed it, or cherished it?"

I glanced at the loving hands still holding tightly the Holy book. He followed my glance and holding up the book asked, "How does Christ feel when we don't even take time to open it? Or when we don't use His gift of repentance, the one He purchased with such a great price? How sad it is when gifts are not received in the same spirit they are given!"

He stood up. He was leaving, making his way slowly down the aisle. He paused just as he reached the front and said, "One last gift. Peace! Peace I leave with you, my peace I give unto you; not as the world giveth, give I unto you. Let not your heart be troubled, neither let it be afraid."

With those words, he was gone. That was fifteen years ago, only a wink in time. But not even an eternity could erase the sermon, or the man.

Costley

Remember When

From *Stillmeadow in December*
Gladys Taber

Something very special happens in December. As Christmas cards and notes arrive, I step briefly from my own life into the lives of people who are dear to me, but far away. And, strangely, I move back in time with old friends. I am glad to know that Charlotte has another grandchild, but I see her as a girl with wind-tossed hair and laughter like golden bells. I am back in the parlor (for we had parlors in my small town), and she is playing by ear on a shiny upright piano. She is always playing "Maple Leaf Rag" because that is what I always ask for. It is good news that Harry has built a new house, but I see him again as a tall, long-legged boy covered with mud and making a touchdown on the football field. Peg is in California; the children are grown up. But I think of the long violet twilights when she walked home with me and then I walked home with her and then we both were roundly scolded by our parents for being late to supper.

As the greeting cards arrive, I put them on two of the mantels, in the corner cupboard where I keep the milk glass, and on the bookshelves. During this festive season I can pause in my daily rounds as the gay Christmas tidings on each card catch my eye.

The whole valley begins to take on a holiday appearance as December goes along. The giant pine at the village center glows with lights. Christmas wreaths blossom on every door. George decorates the market, and Green's store

looks like a Christmas party. The post office is piled so high with packages that I can barely see the heads of the postal workers. No window is without a string of lights, a sprig of green, or a glitter of tinsel.

But I think I must be the first person in the village to put up Christmas trimmings. Erma helps me decorate Stillmeadow with mistletoe, holly, and pine branches, which add a green, spicy touch to the old house. Christmas candles brighten the wide window ledges, but I never put them on the tree, for I am afraid they might start a fire. Bowls of fruit and nuts appear—temporary decorations, for the children start munching and cracking as soon as they arrive for the holiday. The bowl on the coffee bench has to be refilled several times a day.

When it is time to put up the tree, out come the cherished ornaments that have survived a Siamese, a good many cocker puppies, the waving tails of several Irish setters, and various small children who couldn't resist patting shiny balls. Some even decided that a tree was for climbing! We always put our tree in the front living room, and as the gaily wrapped presents are ready, they go under it.

I hope Christmas gifts never go out of style, for they are evidence of loving and caring, which all of us need. I love the excitement that accompanies the opening of boxes—the rustle of tissue paper, the exclamations of surprise and delight, the stepping over toy trains and stuffed toys and educational blocks, the wallet and tie clasp and four ties, the dainty slip and leather gloves and fragrant colognes in pretty bottles. I know some people gladly settle for money, but how prosaic that is! Gifts may be lavish, they may be simple, but it is so nice to be remembered.

There is an old tradition that on Christmas Eve,
the little boy Jesus again walks the earth; and in the old country,
the mother always sets a lighted candle in the window
to light Him on His way.

THE LIGHTED CANDLE

I have no window looking on the street,
Where I might set a candle Christmas Eve,
To light the little Jesus on His way,
For it is said . . . and so I do believe
The little Christ Child walks again on earth,
On this sweet-memoried evening of His birth.

My window looks upon a little lane
Where there are rutted tracks and broken things.
An old gray shed . . . a bit of sagging fence,
So poor, and yet tonight the moonlight flings
A shining banner like a silver haze,
Clothing with beauty all its shabby ways.

And so perhaps if He should come our way,
Along this little frozen path, He might
See beauty in a humble country lane,
So I will pull the curtains back tonight,
And set a candle where its flickering glow
Will make a path of silver in the snow.

Edna Jaques

CHRISTMAS—AND I REMEMBER

'Tis Christmas Eve. Gay little candles burn,
Each haloed with a circlet of pure gold;
Pink waxen angels' gauzy wings unfold.

We children all, mother and father, too,
And still, adoring, in this mystic hour;
Round eyes of blue, small faces flushed with joy—
We feel, but do not understand, its power.

Then childish voices rise in *Stille Nacht*,
While one by one the candles burn away;
The last flame dies, the sweet young voices fade:
But while I live, I keep this blessed day.

Rose Koralewsky

A glowing candle shines from behind the window pane. Photograph by John Gajda/ FPG International.

CANDLESTICKS

by Angela Giovanni

When my grandmother traveled from Greece to America three-quarters of a century ago, she was sixteen years old. She left behind her mother and father, her three sisters, her home, her language and her culture. Her destination was Boston. As many times as I hear the story, I cannot imagine her journey—for not only did she leave her native country for one totally unfamiliar, but she left behind her life as a daughter to become wife to a man she had never met. An arranged marriage brought her to America, a marriage her family knew would be good for her, to a man already established in America, with a home and a business. But, nonetheless, he was a stranger, and a stranger twice her age. Amazingly, the marriage proved to be a good match. Yia Yia and Papa had a long, happy life together, and raised four children, one of whom was my father.

Papa died many years ago, and Yia Yia has carried on. She is devoted to her home, and I have always liked to imagine this devotion stems from the fact that she started that home with nothing, only the scant belongings packed in the single bag that made the trip with her from Greece. She has become an ardent collector over the years—a collector of household items. In particular, she loves candlesticks. At her home in Greece so many years ago, candles were the only form of lighting. And when she left for America, she carried with her a pair of simple ceramic candle-

At Yia Yia's home in Greece so many years ago, candles were the only form of lighting. And when she left for America, she carried with her a pair of simple ceramic candlesticks . . .

sticks, white with roughly painted blue flowers. These candlesticks survived the Atlantic voyage, and, in fact, they have survived the nearly seventy-five years since. They are scratched and chipped and were long ago relegated to a place far back on a shelf. They have been joined through the years by an impressive array of candlesticks in every shape, size, and material. There appears to be no rhyme or reason to Yia Yia's collection of candlesticks. She has brass candlesticks long ago in need of polishing. She has what must be the most ornate candlestick ever made, a single metal piece in the form of a flowering shrub with places for eight candles and enough ornate detail to overshadow the glow of any eight candles. She has glass candlesticks that catch the light and reflect it off in every direction, and ceramic sticks adorned by roses in reds, pinks, and yellows. Yia Yia loves flowers and flourish, and most of her candlesticks are ornate and formal looking, but I did find a few simple terracotta sticks and a pair of beautiful blue colored glass candle holders with simple, elegant lines.

I have always been amazed by Yia Yia's devotion to household items, to her many collections. I admit that sometimes the overwhelming feeling I get in her house is one of clutter, but a patient gaze will reveal treasures. She loves little ceramic flowers and they cover every available flat surface in her living room. She collects Huemmels and also has what must be the world's largest collection of delicate porcelain candy dishes with gold edging. When we were kids, my sister and I would walk through this room quickly, in fear, knowing that the slightest misstep could send some breakable item crashing to the floor. Today, I try to walk through the room slowly—although still very carefully—and to imagine what each collection, each piece, means to her.

I am sure that Yia Yia does not think of herself as a collector of candlesticks. She might not even realize how many she has. When I asked her about them, she waved it off, saying they were just things she had picked up through the years, gifts from friends, finds at church bazaars. But, always looking for order and significance in life, even in Yia Yia's crowded living room, I see in her attachment to her candlesticks a reflection of the feelings of that innocent teenage girl who faced the unknown so bravely, who made a home for herself and her family in a strange land. I like to picture her lighting simple white candles held by those two ancient ceramic candlesticks, thinking about her home in Greece as she set about creating a new home half a world away.

FLICKERING FACTS

If you would like to begin collecting candlesticks, here are some interesting facts:

HISTORY
•Candlesticks are an easy collectible to find. Collectors can focus on silver, glass, wood, pewter, bronze, ceramic, porcelain, iron, or tin.

•Before the 18th century, brass candlesticks were cast in a single piece, making them solid, heavy, and generally quite large. Innovations in metal working eventually allowed for hollow stems, and candlesticks made from smaller, detachable pieces.

•Candlesticks made with solid stems often featured what was called an "economy hole" which made it possible to poke out candle stubs once they had burned below the top of the socket. the stubs could then be remelted and made into new candles by the economy-minded.

•The basic elements of a candlestick are the base, the stem, and the socket, which holds the candle either, or in some older candlesticks, a pricket, on which to impale the wax candle.

These antique candlesticks are an excellent example of bow porcelain.
Image from the London Museum, London, England/Superstock.

CHRISTMAS EVE

A tall red taper burns below
a holly wreath. The crystal snow
flings back the silver light
of stars. Still is the night . . .
and all the world recalls a birth,
an angel's song, and peace on earth.

Virginia Blanck Moore

CANDLELIT HEART

Somewhere across the winter world tonight
You will be hearing chimes that fill the air;
Christmas extends its all-enfolding light
Across the distance . . . something we can share.
You will be singing, just the same as I,
These old familiar songs we know so well,
And you will see these same stars in your sky
And wish upon that brightest one that fell.
I shall remember you and trim my tree,
One shining star upon the topmost bough;
I will hang wreaths of faith that all may see.
Tonight I glimpse beyond the here and now,
And all the years that we must be apart
I keep a candle lighted in my heart.

Mary E. Linton

A young girl admires a flickering candle at Christmas time. Photograph by Jim Whitmer.

Skating

All shod with steel
   We hissed along the polished ice in games
     Confederate, imitative of the chase
     And woodland pleasures,—the resounding horn,
     The pack loud chiming, and the hunted hare.
     So through the darkness and the cold we flew,
    And not a voice was idle: with the din
    Smitten, the precipices rang aloud;
   The leafless trees and every icy crag
  Tinkled like iron; while far distant hills
 Into the tumult sent an alien sound
Of melancholy not unnoticed, while the stars
Eastward were sparkling clear, and in the west
The orange sky of evening died away.
 Not seldom from the uproar I retired
  Into a silent bay, or sportively
   Glanced sideway, leaving the tumultuous throng,
    To cut across the reflex of a star
     That fled, and, flying still before me, gleamed
     Upon the glassy plain: and oftentimes,
      When we had given our bodies to the wind,
      And all the shadowy banks on either side
       Came sweeping through the darkness, spinning still
      The rapid line of motion, then at once
      Have I, reclining back upon my heels,
     Stopped short; yet still the solitary cliffs
    Wheeled by me—even as if the earth had rolled
   With visible motion her diurnal round!
  Behind me did they stretch in solemn train,
 Feebler and feebler, and I stood and watched
Till all was tranquil as a dreamless sleep.

               William Wordsworth

Konstantin Rodko depicts skating on the pond. Superstock Inc. Collection, Jacksonville.

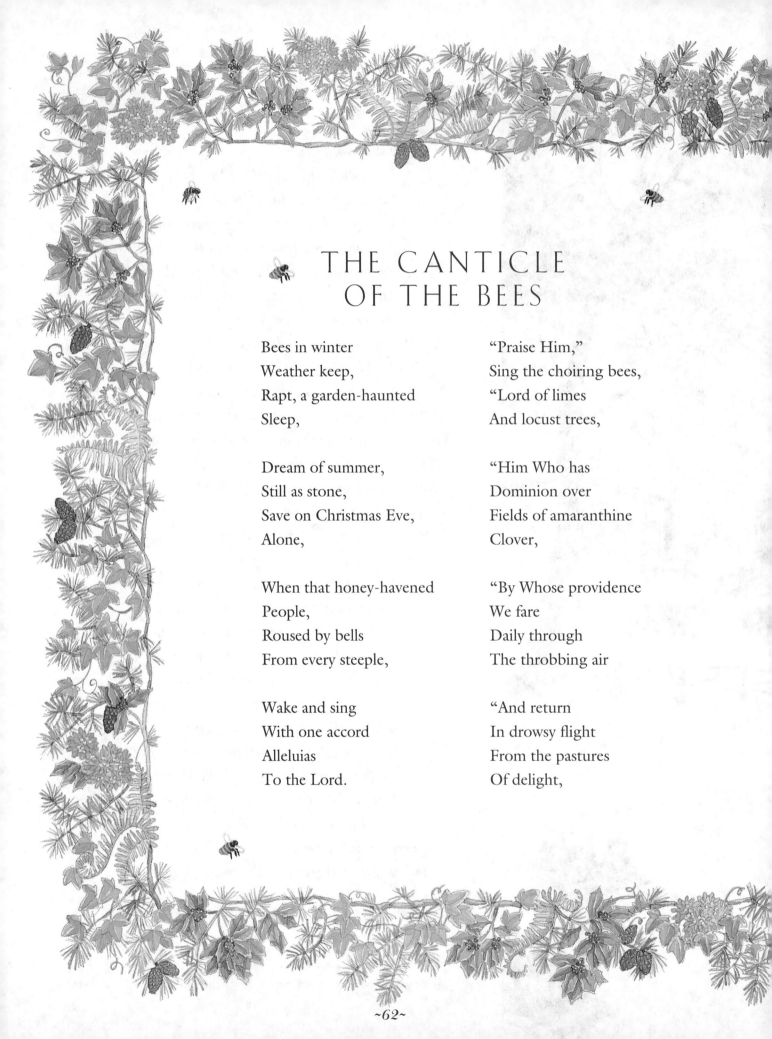

THE CANTICLE
OF THE BEES

Bees in winter
Weather keep,
Rapt, a garden-haunted
Sleep,

Dream of summer,
Still as stone,
Save on Christmas Eve,
Alone,

When that honey-havened
People,
Roused by bells
From every steeple,

Wake and sing
With one accord
Alleluias
To the Lord.

"Praise Him,"
Sing the choiring bees,
"Lord of limes
And locust trees,

"Him Who has
Dominion over
Fields of amaranthine
Clover,

"By Whose providence
We fare
Daily through
The throbbing air

"And return
In drowsy flight
From the pastures
Of delight,

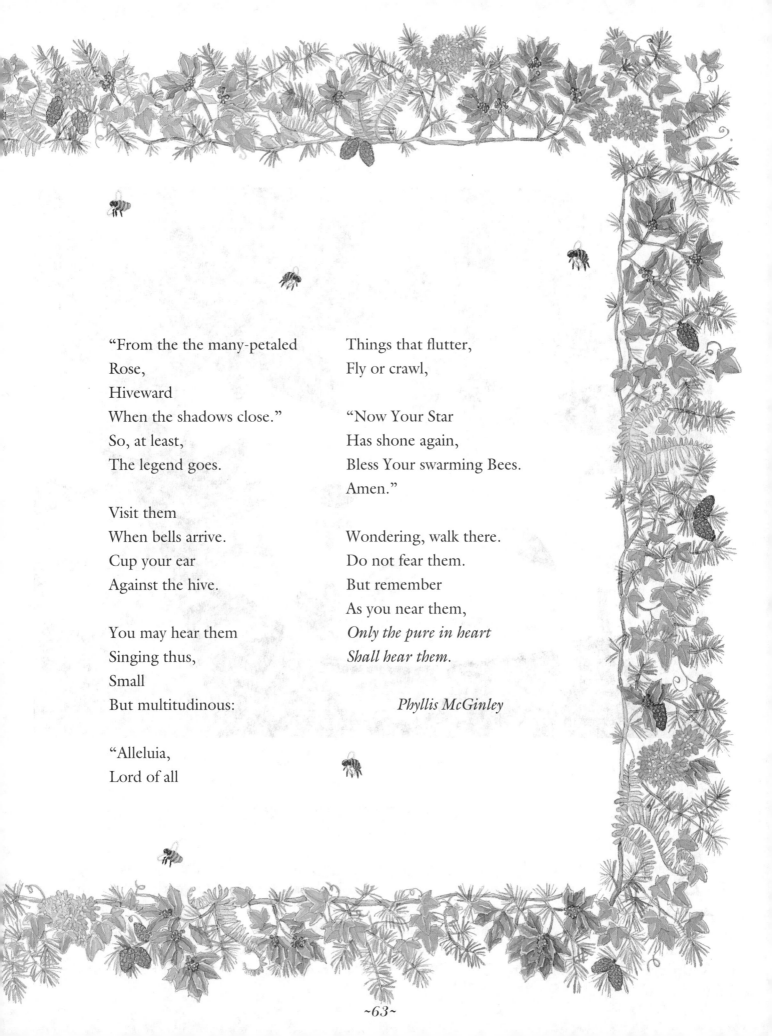

"From the the many-petaled
Rose,
Hiveward
When the shadows close."
So, at least,
The legend goes.

Visit them
When bells arrive.
Cup your ear
Against the hive.

You may hear them
Singing thus,
Small
But multitudinous:

"Alleluia,
Lord of all

Things that flutter,
Fly or crawl,

"Now Your Star
Has shone again,
Bless Your swarming Bees.
Amen."

Wondering, walk there.
Do not fear them.
But remember
As you near them,
Only the pure in heart
Shall hear them.

Phyllis McGinley

A felt Christmas tree skirt can become a treasured heirloom to pass down through the generations. Skirt crafted by Lisa C. Ragan. Photograph by Jerry Koser.

FELT CHRISTMAS TREE SKIRT
Aleah Taylor

A felt Christmas tree skirt was a particularly appealing project for me. When I was a kid, I loved to make things out of felt. There was a five-and-dime store within walking distance of my house and my friend Kathy and I used to walk there with a dollar or two in our pockets and choose five-cent sheets of felt from the bins along the wall in the craft section. I loved the way the felt pieces were stacked neatly on the shelves, arranged in columns according to color and in rows according to shade. I loved the feel of the felt in my hands—soft and sturdy, with nothing frilly or fancy about it. After spending our allotment of nickels, Kathy and I would arrive at my kitchen table with a rich rainbow of colors and get to work cutting and gluing according to that day's whims. Between the time I was eight or nine and the day when my teenage years made such mundane pursuits temporarily uninteresting, I produced a string of felt projects—covered coffee cans, sachets, Christmas ornaments, and wall hangings—that my patient relatives received with a smile on every gift-giving occasion.

The felt I worked with as a child was a synthetic material, but real felt is made entirely from wool. In an ancient process, a tangle of wool is treated with heat, water, and soap to open the natural scales on the individual fibers. As the wool dries, felt-makers pound and roll the fibers, encouraging them to interlock and bind together. The finished product is a dense, warm, water-resistant fabric without equal for cold weather clothing. It is the sturdiest of natural fabrics, but also the softest. And while it does not have the stretch or give for complicated or tailored sewing projects, felt does not pull, pucker, or unravel; it stands up well to simple stitching and never needs hemming or special edging. When I was a girl, I thought the synthetic felt from the five-and-dime was the most wonderful of fabrics; but real wool felt is even better—adding a luxuriousness to the simplicity and sturdiness that attracted me so long ago.

My mentor in all my childhood crafting projects was my mother, herself an accomplished seamstress who was the master of hand and machine sewing and could handle fabrics far less forgiving than felt. Yet she stood by us patiently as we cut and glued and made our first tentative stitches. She provided the pinking shears for decorative edging, and the ribbons scraps and extra buttons we used for adornment. It was as a tribute to her patient guidance that I decided to make a felt Christmas tree skirt this year. But nostalgia only goes so far: no common dime store synthetic felt would do for this project. For my mother's Christmas tree skirt I choose pure wool felt in the richest Christmas reds and greens.

The basic skirt began with two 13 1/2 x 27-inch pieces of green felt. On these I drew an arc from one bottom corner of the long side to the other, and then a second arc beginning 2 1/2 inches from the center and ending the same distance from the center on the opposite side. Picture the shape of a rainbow, with the largest arc reaching from one corner to the next, and the smallest spanning a distance of five inches at the center point of the fabric piece. When the two arcs were complete, I joined them to form a circle, securing one seam with topstitching, and the other with three large buttons. I did the buttonholes on my sewing machine, but they could also be made by hand, or the seam could be joined by topstitching and the buttons added as a decorative touch. I appliqued my skirt with poinsettias cut from red and a deep shade of green. The skirt is the perfect size to fit over one of the popular cone-shaped plastic Christmas tree stands.

The simplicity of this project reminded me of why felt was such an attractive fabric choice for my unrefined cutting and sewing skills all those years ago. But the Christmas tree skirt far out shines those old kitchen-table creations. Real wool felt has a richness that is beyond compare; it just looks and feels like wintertime and Christmas. I can't wait to present it to my mother. I don't know if she remembers those days of felt crafting as warmly as I do, but I hope that this gift will evoke some happy memories for her. Crafts like this one bring joy into my everyday life, and for that, I thank my mother. She taught me to love to create with my hands by letting me work at my own speed and to my own standards. She let me think that that dime store felt was the most luxurious of fabrics, and that my coffee can creations were more beautiful than any gift money could buy.

A SLICE OF LIFE
Edgar A. Guest

A BOY AT CHRISTMAS

If I could have my wish tonight,
    It would not be for wealth or fame,
It would not be for some delight
    That men who live in luxury claim,
But it would be that I might rise
    At three or four A.M. to see,
With eager, happy, boyish eyes,
    My presents on the Christmas tree.
Throughout this world there is no joy,
    I know now I am growing gray,
So rich as being just a boy,
    A little boy on Christmas Day.

I'd like once more to stand and gaze
    Enraptured on a tinseled tree,
With eyes that know just how to blaze,
    A heart still tuned to ecstasy;
I'd like to feel the old delight,
    The surging thrills within me come;
To love a thing with all my might,
    To grasp the pleasure of a drum;
To know the meaning of a toy—
    A meaning lost to minds blasé;
To be just once again a boy,
    A little boy on Christmas Day.

I'd like to see a pair of skates
    The way they looked to me back then,
Before I'd turned from boyhood's gates
    And marched into the world of men;
I'd like to see a jackknife, too,
    With those same eager, dancing eyes
That couldn't fault or blemish view;
    I'd like to feel the same surprise,
The pleasure free from all alloy,
    That has forever passed away,
When I was just a little boy
    And had my faith in Christmas Day.

Oh, little, laughing, roguish lad,
    The king that rules across the sea
Would give his scepter if he had
    Such joy as now belongs to thee!
And beards of gray would give their gold,
    And all the honors they possess,
Once more within their grasp to hold
    Thy present fee of happiness.
Earth sends no greater, surer joy,
    As, too soon, thou, as I, shall say,
Than that of him who is a boy,
    A little boy on Christmas Day.

DECEMBER

Glad Christmas comes, and every hearth
Makes room to give him welcome now,
E'en want will dry its tears in mirth,
And crown him with a holly bough;
Though tramping 'neath a winter sky,
O'er snowy paths and rimy stiles,
The housewife sets her spinning by
To bid him welcome with her smiles.

Each house is swept the day before,
And windows stuck with evergreens,
The snow is besom'd from the door,
And comfort the crowns the cottage scenes.
Gilt holly, with its thorny pricks,
And yew and box, with berries small,
These deck the unused candlesticks,
And pictures hanging by the wall.

Gingerbread men put on their holiday faces. Photograph by Nancy Matthews.

Neighbors resume their annual cheer,
Wishing, with smiles and spirits high,
Glad Christmas and a happy year
To every morning passer-by;
Milkmaids their Christmas journeys go,
Accompanied with favour'd swain;
And children pace the crumpling snow,
To taste their granny's cake again.

The shepherd, now no more afraid,
Since custom doth the chance bestow,
Starts up to kiss the giggling maid
Beneath the branch of mistletoe
That 'neath each cottage beam is seen,
With pearl-like berries shining gay;
The shadow still of what hath been,
Which fashion yearly fades away.

John Clare

Ideals' Family Recipes

Gingerbread People

½ cup margarine or butter
2½ cups all-purpose flour
½ cup granulated sugar
½ cup molasses
1 egg

1 teaspoon baking soda
1 teaspoon ground ginger
½ teaspoon ground cinnamon
½ teaspoon ground cloves
Vanilla-flavored frosting

In a large bowl, beat margarine with an electric mixer on medium to high speed about 30 seconds or until softened. Add about half of the flour and mix well. Add sugar, molasses, egg, baking soda, ginger, cinnamon, and cloves. Beat until thoroughly combined. Stir in the remaining flour. Divide dough in half. Cover and chill about 3 hours or until easy to handle.

Preheat oven to 375° F. Grease a cookie sheet; set aside. On a lightly floured surface, roll each half of dough to ⅛-inch thickness.

Using 3- to 4-inch people-shaped cookie cutters, cut dough into shapes. Place 1 inch apart on the prepared cookie sheet. Bake 5 to 6 minutes or until edges are firm. Cool on cookie sheet 1 minute. Transfer cookies to a wire rack to cool.

When completely cool, decorate with vanilla-flavored frosting. Makes about 3 dozen cookies.

Victoria Richter
Carbondale, Illinois

Grandma's Cranberry-Ginger Pie

One 9-inch prepared pastry for double-crust pie
One 15¼-ounce can crushed pineapple
3 cups cranberries

1¼ cups granulated sugar
¼ cup cornstarch
2 tablespoons finely chopped crystallized ginger

Preheat oven to 375° F. Drain pineapple, reserving juice. Add enough water to the pineapple juice to make 1 cup. In a medium sauce pan, combine cranberries and pineapple juice mixture. Bring to a boil. Reduce heat and simmer, uncovered, about 5 minutes or until cranberries split open. In a small bowl, stir together sugar and cornstarch. Add sugar mixture to cranberries. Cook and stir until bubbly. Remove from heat. Stir in pineapple and ginger.

Line a 9-inch pie plate with half of the

prepared pastry. Transfer cranberry mixture to the pastry-lined pie plate. Trim bottom pastry to ½ inch beyond edge of pie plate. Cut remaining half of prepared pastry into one-inch strips. Place pastry strips on top of pie in a lattice pattern. Seal and crimp edge.

To prevent overbrowning, cover edge of pie with foil. Bake 25 minutes. Remove foil. Bake an additional 20 to 25 minutes or until golden. Cool on a wire rack. Serves 8.

Helen McPhee
Atascadero, California

Spicy Gingersnap Cookies

2¼ cups all-purpose flour
1 cup packed brown sugar
¾ cup shortening
¼ cup molasses
1 egg

1 teaspoon baking soda
1 teaspoon ground ginger
1 teaspoon ground cinnamon
½ teaspoon ground cloves
¼ cup granulated sugar

Preheat oven to 375° F. In a large bowl, place half of the flour. Add the brown sugar, shortening, molasses, egg, baking soda, ginger, cinnamon, and cloves. Beat with an electric mixer on medium to high speed until thoroughly combined, scraping sides of bowl occasionally; stir in the remaining flour.

Shape dough into 1-inch balls; roll in granulated sugar to coat. Place 2 inches apart on an ungreased cookie sheet. Bake 8 to 10 minutes or until edges are set and tops are crackled. Cool on cookie sheet 1 minute. Transfer cookies to a wire rack. Makes about 4 dozen cookies.

Irene Vayndiner
Washington, D.C.

Old-Fashioned Gingerbread

½ cup butter
½ cup granulated sugar
1 egg
2½ cups sifted all-purpose flour

1½ teaspoons baking soda
1 teaspoon ground cinnamon
1 teaspoon ground ginger
½ teaspoon salt

½ cup light molasses
½ cup honey
1 cup hot water
1 teaspoon grated orange zest

Preheat oven to 350° F. In a heavy saucepan, melt butter. Remove from heat and let cool. Add granulated sugar and egg; beat well.

In a large bowl, sift together flour, baking soda, cinnamon, ginger, and salt; set aside. In a separate bowl, combine molasses, honey, hot water, and orange zest. Add the dry and liquid ingredients alternately to the butter mixture until blended. Bake in a greased 9-by-9-by-2-inch pan 1 hour.

Niusia Millman
Bloomington, Indiana

Ginger Crinkle Crisps

2¼ cups all-purpose flour
¼ teaspoon salt
2 teaspoons baking soda
1 teaspoon ground ginger

1 teaspoon ground cinnamon
½ teaspoon ground cloves
1 cup packed brown sugar
¾ cup shortening

¼ cup molasses
1 egg
granulated sugar

Preheat oven to 375° F. In a large bowl, stir together the flour, salt, baking soda, ginger, cinnamon, and cloves; set aside. In a separate bowl, combine the brown sugar, shortening, molasses, and egg; beat well. Add dry ingredients to molasses mixture, beating well. Shape dough into 1-inch balls; roll in granulated sugar to coat. Place balls 2 inches apart on an ungreased cookie sheet. Bake 10 minutes. Transfer cookies to a wire rack to cool. Makes 4 dozen cookies.

Mary Catherine Paden
Hanford, California

LEGENDARY AMERICANS

NANCY J. SKARMEAS

FLORENCE SABIN

Late in her life, Florence Sabin designed a bookplate to be placed inside her most cherished volumes. It featured a microscope—symbolic of her long career as a medical researcher—and a quote by Leonardo da Vinci. "Thou, O God," the line read, "dost sell unto us all good things at the price of labor." Da Vinci's words were Sabin's credo; for hers was truly a life devoted to work. But Florence Sabin was not a common workaholic devoted to personal gain. She was a doctor, a brilliant researcher, a beloved teacher, and a crusader for

public health; and the "good things" she sought to earn with her labor were nothing less than the improved health and well being of mankind.

Sabin was born in Central City, Colorado, in 1871. Her father was a miner and her mother a teacher. Both had come west independently from eastern roots to seek a better life. Florence and her sister Mary spent their early childhood in Colorado, and after their mother's death in 1878, lived alternately in Illinois with an aunt and uncle, in Vermont with their grandparents, and back in Colorado with their father. Both Sabin sisters defied convention by pursuing higher education, and by choosing careers and independence over marriage and family and the subservience that these implied for women at the turn of the twentieth century in America. Mary set her sights on a career as a teacher, and Florence determined that she would be a doctor.

Florence Sabin liked to say that being female was no handicap to her as she pursued her career, but the truth is, obstacles existed, she simply chose not to be discouraged or distracted by them. And she also made very wise choices. For her undergraduate studies, Sabin chose Smith College, the first American college to offer advanced degrees to women and a school whose focus was on providing its all-female student body with an education on par with that of the best men's schools of the day. For medical school, she selected Johns Hopkins in Baltimore. The school had only recently been founded when Sabin applied, financed by a group of women intent upon opening up the medical professions to women. At Johns Hopkins, Sabin was one of fifteen women in a class of forty-two, and while she endured some skepticism from the male students and doctors, she had the full support of the school administration. Sabin was a bright and driven student, but her most valuable attribute as she struggled to defy the conventions that kept women out of the medical field was her ability to focus not on what the world was doing to hold her back, but on what she must do to propel herself forward.

Sabin received her medical degree in 1900. She chose not to go into clinical practice, but to focus her work on research. She made her decision based upon the empirical evidence, just as she had done throughout her life, inside and outside the laboratory. As a young girl, Sabin had dreamed of becoming a professional musician. But when a fellow student at her boarding school remarked that her playing was hardly of the caliber to earn a living, Sabin did not react defensively to the criticism, but instead considered the truth of the statement and revised her plans. Acknowledging her lifelong interest in science, and her love of experiments and detail, she gave up the piano to concentrate more on her studies in the sciences. She applied the same objectivity to her decision to become a research physician. After a particularly trying two months of obstetrical internship at Johns Hopkins, Sabin recognized that her character was not suited to the fast-paced and unpredictable world of the hospital, but more at home in the quiet and predictable atmosphere of the research lab. Her decision did not reflect a lack of concern for patients, but a true devotion to them. The vision that inspired her career was of "a time when men and women will live their allotted space quietly, without illness, free from pain." It was in the lab that she set out to fulfill that vision.

For twenty-five years, Sabin remained at Johns Hopkins as a researcher and a teacher. She performed groundbreaking research on the lymphatic system and also helped develop new techniques for studying blood cells in live tissue. Her teaching style was revolutionary. She encouraged her students to work on their own and in groups to discover truths and facts by themselves through experimentation. She also tore up her lecture notes after each semester, forcing herself to tackle each topic anew with every new group of students. Sabin's presence and success at Johns Hopkins pushed forward the cause of women in medical schools and the medical professions, and her devotion and skill inspired countless students, male and female, to greater accomplishment in the sciences.

In 1925, she accepted a position at the Rockefeller Institute for Medial Research in New York City. For the next thirteen years, Sabin researched infectious diseases, in particular tuberculosis. Her work was done quietly, and she never had the chance to attach her name to a cure or any other great, newsworthy discovery; but she herself understood the fact that behind every such moment of discovery in medical science were endless hours of laboratory work by tireless researchers like herself. She was happy to remain busily anonymous.

Sabin entered her first period of retirement in 1938, and settled back in Denver with her sister Mary. She was restless, however, and by 1944, began working again, this time for the state of Colorado. Chosen to serve on a state commission on public health, Sabin turned her devotion and energy to improving living conditions for the citizens of her native state. She improved standards for safe beef and milk, and she rid the city of rat problems, and improved the sewage system. For the first time in her life, Sabin became a public figure, speaking to Coloradans about health issues, and even bringing medical tests and information directly to the people through free clinics and screenings. When she retired from her work in Colorado, the state was a safer, healthy place to live, and Florence Sabin was among the most admired women, or men, in the state. Sabin died in Denver in 1953. Five years later, a statue was dedicated to her memory in Statuary Hall at the Capitol building in Washington, D. C.

Florence Sabin's list of firsts is quite impressive. She was the first woman on the faculty at Johns Hopkins Medical School, the first female president of the American Association of Anatomists, the first woman elected to the National Academy of Sciences, the first recipient of the Jane Addams Medal for distinguished service by an American woman. But it a disservice to view her success as that of a woman in a man's world, or to evaluate her life and career by a list of public accolades and honors. Florence Sabin was . a scientist of brilliance and commitment, a doctor devoted to the health and well-being of her fellow citizens. She was woman—a human—who worked hard every day of her life to make a positive difference in her world and achieved extraordinary success.

Nancy Skarmeas is a book editor and mother of a toddler, Gordon, who keeps her and her husband quite busy at their home in New Hampshire. Her Greek and Irish ancestry has fostered a lifelong interest in research and history.

FIRESIDE DREAMS

When snow's piled high in field and tree and frost on windows prey,
    The fireside is a pleasant place to spend a winter's day.
I like to draw my chair up close and turn the lights down low
    Then watch the flames caress the logs amid the embers' glow.

The shadows leap about the room and dance upon the wall
    As if they'd been invited to the grandest kind of ball.
The music of the crackling wood is like a serenade,
    And nerves begin relaxing as life's tensions start to fade.

It's then that Morpheus greets me and bids me be his guest,
    And I accept the invitation with head resting on my chest.
Then I enter into dreamland with its many fantasies
    And care nothing for the present with its stark realities.

So let winter wreak its fury and blow its icy chill
    And the snow pile high as mountains upon my windowsill.
As long as I have ample logs to help withstand the tide,
    I'll sit and dream the livelong day beside my fireside.

Ned Nichols

SAFE

Come, stir the fire,
The lamps unlit
Leave, while we sit
Close to the glow,
And fire and shadow flit
About the room, and fight
For love of it.

Cold winds blow
Whirling in the drear
Night outside; the blaze
Uncoils its tentacles, and here
We in a dream-daze
With the lamps unlit,
Safe in firelight sit.

James Walker

The country fireplace and Christmas decor makes for a welcoming sight. Photograph by Jessie Walker.

The FDR Memorial is a new addition to the historical landscape of Washington D.C.
Photograph by Rosa Wilson/Department of the Interior.

DECEMBER 7, 1941

Yesterday, December 7, 1941—a date which will live in infamy—the United States of America was suddenly and deliberately attacked by naval and air forces of the empire of Japan.

The United States was at peace with that nation and, at the solicitation of Japan, was still in conversation with its government and its emperor looking toward the maintenance of peace in the Pacific. Indeed, one hour after Japanese air squadrons had commenced bombing in Oahu, the Japanese ambassador to the United States and his colleague delivered to the secretary of state a formal reply to a recent American message. While this reply stated that it seemed useless to continue the existing diplomatic negotiations, it contained no threat or hint of war or armed attack. It will be recorded that the distance of Hawaii from Japan makes it obvious that the attack was deliberately planned many days or even weeks ago. During the intervening time the Japanese government has deliberately sought to deceive the United States by false statements and expressions of hope and continued peace.

The attack yesterday on the Hawaiian Islands has caused severe damage to American naval and military forces. Very many American lives have been lost. In addition American ships have been reported torpedoed on the high seas between San Francisco and Honolulu.

Yesterday the Japanese government also launched an attack against Malaya. Last night, Japanese forces attacked Hong Kong. Last night, Japanese forces attacked Guam. Last night, Japanese forces attacked the Philippine Islands. Last night, the Japanese attacked Wake Island. This morning, the Japanese attacked Midway Island.

Japan has therefore undertaken a surprise offensive extending throughout the Pacific area. The facts of yesterday and today speak for themselves. The people of the United States have already formed their opinions and well understand the implications to the very life and safety of our nation.

As commander in chief of the Army and Navy, I have directed that all measures be taken for our defense.

Always will we remember the character of the onslaught against us. No matter how long it may take to overcome this premeditated invasion, the American people in their righteous might will win through to absolute victory. I believe I interpret the will of the Congress and of the people when I assert that we will not only defend ourselves to the uttermost but will make certain that this form of treachery shall never endanger us again.

Hostilities exist. There is no blinking at the fact that our people, our territory, and our interests are in grave danger. With confidence in our armed forces—with the unbounding determination of our people—we will gain the inevitable triumph, so help us God. I ask that the Congress declare that since the unprovoked and dastardly attack by Japan on Sunday, December 7, 1941, a state of war has existed between the United States and the Japanese Empire.

President Franklin D. Roosevelt
December 8, 1941

ABOUT THE TEXT

On the morning of Sunday, December 7, 1941, the first wave of more than 300 Japanese warplanes roared over the northern tip of the Hawaiian island of Oahu, headed toward the American naval base at Pearl Harbor. Minutes before 8 a.m., the Japanese planes unleashed a brutal, surprise attack on the ships of the U.S. Pacific Fleet and the planes at the adjoining airfields. The attack left nearly 3,500 sailors, soldiers, and civilians dead. President Roosevelt responded to the attack with a declaration of war.

Favorite Season

There is a coziness
  About the wintertime
When whirling snowflakes scurry
  And huge back-logs blaze;
I think that I would miss this
  In a southern clime
That brings no change
  From endless summer, sunny days.

And have you noticed
  How a dazzling, gay snowstorm
Brings quick and friendly greetings
  With a wave and shout
From neighbors and from strangers?
  There is something warm
And friendly about wintertime,
  Within, without.

I never have liked the staleness,
  And when seasons change
I welcome them, for each one brings
  Its own bequest.
Don't tell the other seasons,
  They might think it strange—
But just at present
  I like wintertime the best.

Isla Paschal Richardson

*A water fall carves its way through the rocky terrain of Adams Falls,
Riceketts Glen State Park, Pennsylvania.
Photograph by Gene Ahrens.*

TRAVELER'S *Diary*

from NINE POUNDS OF LUGGAGE
Maude Parrish

I had a little money, and my banjo. I didn't know what I'd do when the money ran out, but I went anyway, to Seattle, and quick as a wink I got a passage on a boat to Alaska. The air was full of the Klondyke. The lure of adventure pulled me aboard and the tied-down feeling stayed ashore.

Here I saw people I could understand. Here were those in the flesh who had filled my imagination, who had lived and traveled in my mental map of Old Mother Earth. . . . Those miners, prospectors, contractors, adventurers, gamblers; those other mysterious characters whose business it would be difficult to figure, suited my dream. There were a few women on the boat, planning to start hotels or restaurants, and one or two like myself who just wanted to see what the Klondyke had in store for them. There were no prospectors' wives, because prospectors didn't have wives—not to mention. But no matter who they were or where they were from, both old and young had the spirit I admired.

From Skadway I went over the Pass to White Horse, part of the way hiking and part by the dog team. I really felt free then in that country! From there by dog team five hundred miles to Dawson. Dogs and people were bursting to get into that capital of frozen northland. I arrived with but ten dollars, but Mr. Rockefeller himself never felt richer. In that exhilarating atmosphere, I'd have bet I could clear the mountains with a hop, skip, and jump. The very air was electric, and the people were electric too, one hundred per cent alive, whatever else ailed them. What if they had run away from wives or husbands, conventions and restrictions? The call of adventure, the call of the wild, was in most of them, no matter what they were doing.

Maud Parrish boasts in her memoirs that she traveled around the world no less than sixteen times with nothing but "nine pounds of luggage," as she titled her memoirs, and a banjo. In Alaska, where Parrish met fellow adventurers with whom she felt she could identify, she made stops in Dawson City, Yukon, and Nome. The traveling life suited Parrish well; she died at age ninety-eight.

The snowy peaks of Hubbard Glacier and the St. Elias Mountain Range create a breathtaking view. Photograph by Uniphoto.

BEAUTY OF A
WINTER NIGHT

On a dark and placid night
In the midst of winter's cold
Shone the stars from heaven high
Like bright lamps of purest gold.

Stately trees trimmed silver-white
From the rage of winter storms
Glistened in the starry night
In majestic, eerie form.

All about there was a glow
Steeped in solemnness profound;
'Twas a beauty deep and grave
That this winter walker found.

George R. Kossik

Christmas lights on an old covered bridge near Waupaca, Wisconsin reflect gently on the waters below. Photograph by Ken Dequaine.